Do You Come Here Often?

Do You Come Here Often?

A Failure's Guide
to Flirting

TRACEY TURNER

First published in 2004 by
Prion
an imprint of the
Carlton Publishing Group
20 Mortimer Street
London W1T 3JW

Text copyright © Tracey Turner 2002

ISBN 1-85375-494-3

A catalogue record of this book can be obtained from the
British Library

Printed and bound in Great Britain
by Mackays

CONTENTS

Introduction

What is flirting exactly? Why do people who are good at it seem to be happier, more confident, less prone to public humiliation? Can it be learned, or is it a gift?

As a flirting failure, these are questions I often ponder. Good flirts get dates (real ones! Often!), compliments, huge bouquets of flowers ... it seems they lead charmed lives. The rest of us get ignored, rejected, parking tickets and herpes ... if we're lucky.

Since you're reading this book, you've probably asked yourself the same questions (though it's possible you're slightly less prone to morbid negativity and exaggeration). If you feel you are a non-flirt, it might well be that you also moan constantly about the men or women you meet (obviously, which you moan about depends on which you're interested in), and feel that undesirable types are strangely drawn to you...

Undesirable Types Strangely Drawn to Flirting Failures

★ Very drunk people (usually men) who wonder out loud if you might be desperate enough to sleep with them.

★ People with no discernible social skills.

★ Single people who are clearly deeply in love with themselves.

★ Shallow, offensive, sexist reptiles.

★ Single women transparently feigning interest in football or similar in tragic attempt to ingratiate themselves with men.

★ Married people who have recently completed extension/done their own conveyancing/similar.

★ Pretentious gits.

★ Sleazy types who are obviously married and looking for an affair.

★ Gropers.

Of course, these people might well have hidden depths and no doubt are all really nice once you get to know them. But, let's be honest, we'd all really much rather be talking to someone witty, amusing, sensitive and intelligent, with a well-developed social conscience and interests and opinions that mirror our own.

Don't get me wrong. I'm not suggesting for a second that I see flirting as the first rung on the glorious Ladder to Coupledom. I'm sure that one day something bizarre will happen to my brain and I'll feel like spending every weekend in B&Q, but for the moment I'm quite happy being single. It's just that it would be nice not to experience crippling paranoia at almost every social event where I know less than half the people there.

I'm sure we'd all like to be able to mingle effortlessly (having made an impactful entrance that sends a ripple around the room) and charm and be charmed by everyone we meet. How wonderful it would be not only to avoid those embarrassed silences that can descend like freezing fog, but also to hold fascinating and witty conversations with interesting people. However, the grim reality is that, far from being charmed, a female Flirting Failure will often find herself in a corner at a party with a reptilian groper. While she is contemplating various escape plans, and seriously considering the window, several desirable men are flocking, seemingly unbidden, to other women in the room – women, I might add, who do not fall into the category of Raving Beauty. Male Flirting Failures (when they are not part of large, slow-moving herds) are likely to find themselves similarly trapped, perhaps by someone prone to long discursions about property prices.

By the way, I should point out that, for the purposes of this book, the term 'Flirting Failure' or 'failed flirt' refers to lovely people like us who are bright and well-adjusted and have plenty of friends. None of us actually *is* the pretentious git, the groper or the sexist reptile. Although the above are all, technically, Flirting Failures too, they have far more immediate and worrying problems.

So what are the secrets of flirting? What are the mysterious rules and techniques that successful flirts all seem to know about? Can Flirting Failures be turned into successful flirts, and never again fall prey to an Undesirable Type? I decided to find out, and this book is the result – a guide to what flirting is, how to do it, where to do it and who to do it with ... written for (and by) the complete failure.

But first, try this simple test to find out whether or not you really need this book:

Are You a Flirting Failure?

1. When talking to someone you've never met before, do you often feel that...
a) People instinctively like and trust you?
b) You're boring them rigid?

2. How would you describe your appearance?

a) Attractive?

b) Hideous?

3. How often do you make an effort to meet new people?

a) At least once a week.

b) As little as possible.

4. Which of the following most closely describes you?

a) Happy, confident, popular socialite.

b) Friendless depressive.

5. Which of these famous quotations do you most agree with?

a) 'Strangers are just friends you haven't met yet.'

b) 'Hell is other people.'

6. You have just arrived at a party where you know very few people. Do you...

a) immediately make eye contact with the best-looking person in the room and confidently introduce yourself?

b) immediately feel like a boring, unattractive half-wit and spend the evening cowering?

7. Where do you feel most confident?
a) In a large crowd.
b) Completely alone.

8. When you find someone attractive, do you:
a) Assume that he or she will find you attractive too and make an effort to get acquainted?
b) Assume that he or she is out of your league and keep away to avoid abject humiliation?

9. Which of the following do you think is socially acceptable?
a) Stalking.
b) Knife-wielding.

10. Do attractive people flock to you and fawn upon you?
a) Yes.
b) No.

Results

Mostly **a)s**: You are not a Flirting Failure. But you would be surprised by how few people really like you.

Mostly **b)s**: Need I say more? Read on...

Question 9: This is a trick question designed to weed out undesirable readers. If you answered yes to either option, please leave this book immediately.

WHAT IS FLIRTING, AND CAN ANYONE DO IT?

Having carried out an extensive survey, I can only conclude that most of us are pretty confused about what flirting is. If only we lived in the eighteenth century. Things were so much more straightforward then, and everyone knew that flirting was all about hankies and fans: a woman would drop her hanky whenever she saw a man she fancied, and if the man swept up the hanky in a gallant sort of way it meant he returned the compliment. Alternatively, people used a complex form of semaphore involving fans to signal their sexual interest.

Mind you, it's worth bearing in mind that this kind of behaviour was restricted to the upper classes – in those days fans and hankies were items the common people could only dream about, and if you were an ordinary female of child-bearing age you were doing well if you could forage enough root vegetables to feed your ever-growing brood of screaming, sickly infants. Also, whether you were a *comte* or a *paysan* (obviously you'd be French, everyone was in those days) there'd be no antibiotics to cure your running sores, smallpox, syphilis or any of the other potentially fatal and highly contagious diseases which were rife at the time. So you'd be lucky if you weren't too dead to be concerning yourself with fan semaphore and hanky dropping. Now I come to think about it, thank god we don't live in the eighteenth century – flirting might be more difficult to interpret today but at least we have an average life expectancy of over 45.

But back to the survey, which clearly revealed a high level of complete bewilderment on the subject of flirting amongst the public at large:

85% of interviewees were absolutely confident that they weren't at all sure what flirting was.

9% thought they were being propositioned.

77% said they knew several flirts, but were unable to define meaning of term.

12% said they were flirts themselves.

12% were incapable of rational thought.

36% thought flirting should be taught in schools.

49% saw flirting as manipulative.

4% saw flirting as work of Satan.

Of the **85%** who weren't at all sure what flirting was:

32% suggested it meant 'acting available'.

25% thought it was something to do with getting dates.

18% suggested it was something people do to get sex, though weren't sure what.

16% thought it involved flattery and generally toying with people's affections.

7% assumed it had died out in the eighteenth century.

2% had it confused with fellatio.

The evidence of the poll, coupled with results of nationwide focus groups, leads overwhelmingly and inevitably to the conclusion that a worryingly large portion of the population are Flirting Failures (see graph opposite).

As these shocking statistics reveal, a lot of people think of flirting as manipulative, sneaky, or, in a very few cases, the work of Beelzebub himself. Having looked into the subject in detail, I came to the conclusion that this is because there are people about

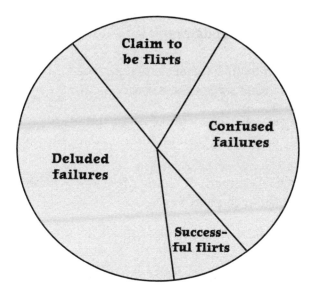

Statistics supplied by the Office of Fair Flirting © 1973.

who call themselves flirts, but are not really flirts at all and are giving flirting a bad name. These impostors include:

★ People (sadly, most often women) who undergo a personality change whenever there's someone they fancy around, instantly losing at least 50 IQ points and commonly regressing to childish giggling.

★ Habitual users of breathtakingly unfunny double-entendres.

★ People (often men) who flatter slimily and indiscriminately.

★ *Blind Date* contestants.

★ Smarmy types.

★ The kind of people who touch your knee 'by accident' a lot – most commonly seen in the workplace.

Makes you shudder, doesn't it? It's small wonder that so many people recoil in horror when you mention flirting. Flirting impostors are often to be found telling anyone who will listen how good at flirting they are. Sadly, as is plainly evident to almost everyone but them, they are very wrong indeed. These people are enough to make anyone's blood run cold, and we'll be desperately trying to find ways of avoiding them later on in this book.

A fairly high proportion of respondents in the survey felt that the purpose of flirting is to get what you want from other people, which is another reason why flirting has a bad name. The whole point of flirting is that it shouldn't be done for a reason – otherwise it's not flirting. So beware if you think you're flirting, but at the back of your mind is one of the following:

★ Hoping for uninhibited, prolonged and energetic sex (or any kind).

★ Hoping to find mother/father of future offspring.

★ Boredom.

★ Seeking attention due to emotional starvation as a child.

★ Attempting to steal someone else's date in revenge attempt.

★ Needing someone willing to buy you

drinks/give lift home due to lack of cash.

★ Needing someone to take to friend's wedding or other social event where coupledom is required.

★ Seeking another initiate for cult.

★ Seeking promotion/pay rise/grope in stationery cupboard/other work-related goal.

If any of these apply to you, you're not really flirting at all (and quite possibly should seek professional help).

So come on, then – what is it?

1. Flirting is engaged in by two consenting adults.

2. It acknowledges the fact that both parties quite fancy one another ...

3. ... but does so in a light-hearted way.

4. It is subtle.

5. It has no agenda, other than for both participants to have a nice time.

6. There are no age or height restrictions.

7. Hurray.

There we are, that was easy, wasn't it? Of course, different people define flirting in all sorts of different ways, but I'd argue that it's a big mistake to include a purpose (apart from enjoying yourself) as part of the definition. The most important thing about flirting is that it's supposed to be fun and spontaneous. (This, after all, was the whole point of the exercise: avoid getting stuck in corner with undesirable types and meet many interesting people instead.) It's totally non-serious, it's not premeditated, you're not out to get anything and your expectations are zero. And there's something else that perhaps should be pointed out at this stage: double entendres are not clever, they're not funny and they're definitely not subtle – they are not the mark of a true flirt.

If you want to be a successful flirt, there's absolutely no point in grimly gritting your teeth, rolling up your sleeves and trying to get the whole thing over with so that you can move on to the even more serious business of The First Date (and, presumably, ultimately moving on to the dizzying excitement of spending your weekends with a pot of emulsion). Apart from the fact that this approach doesn't sound like a barrel of laughs, there is the very real danger that the Whiff of Desperation will sneak in – imperceptible at first, but gradually permeating the atmosphere until any chance you might have had is irrevocably lost. We'll be returning to the Whiff later on – possibly more often than necessary, but personally I don't think it can be emphasised enough.

This was the definition I had in mind when I set out on my quest for flirting success. Being good at flirting means the world becomes a sunnier place. Good flirts tend to be charming not only to people they find attractive, but to everyone (as a natural consequence). No one could really argue that being nice to people and making them feel good about themselves could possibly be anything but a good thing.

But first, in case you were wondering about the reference to *Blind Date* earlier on...

Why Flirting and *Blind Date* are Very Different Things

What happens on *Blind Date* itself can sometimes – though very rarely – be described as flirting. The part I really have in mind, however, is the bit where one of the three *gorgeous* lads/lasses gets chosen by the *gorgeous* lad/lass on the other side of the screen. Here is a typical transcript from the show:

Gorgeous lad:

'Hello, Cilla, my name's Steve and I'm from HULL! [Huge cheers from audience who obviously see this as great achievement.] Question one to number one: I'm like a Ferrari, because I'm expensive, sleek and I go like the clappers. If you were a type of car, what would it be, and why?'

Gorgeous lass:
'Well, Steve, I'd have to be a motorbike because I like to have something big throbbing between my thighs! But I'd love to get my hands on your gear stick and *drive you wild*!'

Possibly (though not necessarily) the most cringe-making element of the above exchange is the fact that both questions and answers have obviously been prepared in advance. Not only is it not spontaneous, but everyone's cards (so to speak) are very clearly laid on the table, and note the use of flagrant sexual innuendo. Need I say more?

Keeping this in mind as a grim example of how not to behave, the next question is...

Can Anyone Learn To Flirt?

As the survey revealed, most people (myself included) think they're Flirting

Failures. And even the ones who think they can flirt often can't. Which means that the vast majority of the population is totally unable to flirt. But is it possible to learn? Is it like swimming – some people are naturally good at it, but everyone can be taught how to do front crawl with time, effort and a good teacher? Or will there always be those of us permanently condemned to social doggie-paddle?

There are plenty of books available on the subject of flirting. Not surprisingly, all of them say that, yes! Anyone can be a fantastic flirt – just go for it! etc, etc, ad nauseam. However, I would point out that there are things which will stop people from wanting to get involved in a flirtatious encounter (or indeed a two-second conversation) with you. These include:

✗ Public nose-picking/farting.

✗ Body odour/halitosis.

✗ Tendency to touch/manipulate own genitals in public.

✗ Suspicious stains on clothing.

✗ Eating and talking at same time.

✗ Craven hand-wringing/drooling.

✗ Any habit from a bygone era, including snuff-taking, chewing tobacco, spitting.

✗ Rhythmic rocking and fixed stare.

The first step on the road to successful flirting is therefore to identify and eradicate any antisocial habits or psychotic tendencies you might have. In some cases this may take years of therapy, but it will be worth it and is absolutely necessary before you start. In my case, just eighteen months of aversion therapy cured me of my unappealing addiction to crispy pork scratchings and I can honestly say that I haven't looked back since.

How to Flirt — in Ten Easy Lessons

There is no shortage of places to find advice on how to flirt, and I decided to begin my quest by trawling through as many books and websites on the subject as I could find. I quickly discovered that flirting advice is an area of publishing that knows no subtlety in terms of its titles. The most toe-curling were *How to Titillate and Captivate!*, *Love's Most Amusing Sport*, and *Bedroom Eyes: The Secrets of Allure*. If they don't send a shiver down your spine, you must be either impervious to pain or a romantic novelist.

But how was I to go into a bookshop and pay for lots of books on the same rather embarrassing subject with my head held high, and with the risk of meeting someone I knew hanging over me like the sword of Damocles? I seriously considered theft for a while, but the consequences of getting arrested for stealing seven books about flirting were even more dreadful than the horrible prospect of bumping into an acquaintance and watching the pity in his/her eyes as I explained that this was *research*. (Imagine the headlines in the local paper: Social

Pariah Helps Herself to Self-Help in Desperate Bid for Boyfriend.)

I ended up persuading a much more courageous friend to buy some of the books for me – she thought the whole thing was hilarious and had to be restrained from reading passages aloud on the bus on the way home. (And I wonder why I'm a flirting failure?)

So it was that, heavily disguised and with the front door firmly bolted and barred, I hunched over dodgily titled books or sat in the dim light of the computer screen and tried to glean the mythical secrets of flirting.

You might have read or heard flirting tips like, 'wear something eye-catching close to your neck,' or, 'always carry something interesting or unusual with you.' It's advice like this that makes it seem as though learning and following a number of complicated rules about behaviour and dress (known only to a select few), and perhaps undergoing some form of initiation ceremony, will turn you from an abject failure into an overnight flirting success. But before you rush out and buy a revolving bow-tie and a stuffed ferret, it's worth having a closer look. Chapters four, five and six reveal many and various flirting techniques and tips (from supposedly successful flirts) on the following subjects:

★ Body language – eye contact, handshakes, postural echo and a little known fact about the Greeks and the Ethiopians.

★ Verbal communication – opening lines, flattery, and a hearty laugh at chat-up lines.

★ Appearance – and some bizarre advice about what to wear (which I think we can safely ignore).

But first, it's time to look at the grim results of my own tragic flirting attempts...

FLIRTING WITH DISASTER

The final stage of my research on flirting is our starting point. It was the part I'd been dreading: going out and attempting to flirt myself. Not laughing at other people, not reading books on the subject, but venturing into the real world and putting theory into practice. At this point I had read and inwardly digested what felt like the accumulated flirting wisdom of the Western world. But now was the time to use all the tips and advice I'd heard and get out there and do my bit for the good of Failed Flirts everywhere. It is my sad duty to relate what happened...

How Not to Flirt 1:
Get Unspeakably Drunk

Location: House-party where I knew only a few people.

What happened: The evening started off well. Having chatted to the people I knew, I found myself (more by luck than judgement) talking to a tree surgeon from Nottingham with a definite twinkle in his eye. It was at this point that a man burst through the door wearing a crazed expression, gleefully proffering a bottle of evil-looking liquid and announcing, 'I've brought some absinthe – it gets you really twisted!' I smiled wryly at my new friend, cradling my second glass of red wine and thinking, 'Well, I won't be drinking any of *that* this evening.'

Quite how the intervening time passed remains something of a mystery, but several hours and many glasses of wine later I was in the kitchen drinking absinthe with the man with the crazed expression. I'm not sure whether or not 'twisted' is an accurate description of my condition, but it sounds appropriate. Not long afterwards I was violently sick in the kitchen sink (reasons for choice of receptacle unclear), regarded with some horror by onlookers. I'm pretty sure that the tree surgeon was one of them.

Marks out of ten: Minus five hundred million.

Mitigating circumstances: The party was held not long before Christmas – a time, you have to admit, when people are more than usually inclined to throw caution to the wind, and over-indulgence is not uncommon.

The moral of the story: Well, I think it's fairly obvious, isn't it?

Repercussions: Disastrous hangover of epic proportions with attendant self-loathing etc. Thankfully not shunned by understanding friends who were holding the party, but have been wary ever since of meeting any of their other friends who might have been present. The tree surgeon has not been heard of since.

How Not to Flirt 2:
Chat room Cowardice

Location: Somewhere in cyberspace.

What happened: After the above attempt at flirting in the real world, I decided to try it virtually. (Which in itself is a sign of total cowardice, but it gets worse.) I told myself that this was in the interests of research, since the chat room is an environment where you can't read body language or intonation. I should start by explaining what happens: you find a flirting website (there are lots) that has a chat room element, then you choose a name and an image (or 'avatar') which you can move about the screen. Then you are unceremoniously dumped in the chat room with other labelled avatars (with whom you can conduct typed conversations), who are really a variety of different sad individuals hunched over computers all around the world intent on striking up virtual sexual encounters. Yes, the Internet is a wonderful thing.

For the first three attempts I couldn't actually bring myself to say anything at all before hurriedly disconnecting from the site in panic. (Another avatar would say 'Hi!' and I would just run away from the computer. No, I'm not proud of it.) Finally I plucked up the courage to say 'Hello!' back – of course, the other avatars couldn't read the *emotional* meaning of my greeting (see page 73) and so didn't realise that I was whimpering with embarrassment. I should explain at this point that the one fun element of all this was choosing different avatars and names (otherwise the other people in the chat room might have recognised me), and I had a variety – at one point I was a blonde called Ursula who I'd decided was going to be rather serious and Teutonic, but unfortunately someone spoke to me in

German after I'd announced I was from the Swiss Alps ... so I had to run away.

When I finally did manage some kind of conversation – and I tried several times – I realised that exchanges would follow a pattern: I'd be asked a few innocent (though sometimes rather bizarre) questions, then someone would suggest going to a one-to-one chat room, where they would enquire as to my bra size or whether I was wearing panties. At which point, that's right, I would run away.

Marks out of ten: One. (For effort?)

Mitigating circumstances: None, unless being a total coward counts.

The moral of the story: It's really not difficult to conclude that, where chat rooms are concerned, 'flirting' is a euphemism. Naturally, these places are havens for sexually frustrated people around the world who are drawn by the idea of pretending to be a tall, dark, muscle-bound hunk called Rod. I was an idiot as well as a coward.

Repercussions: Every time I connect to a website I shudder involuntarily.

How not to Flirt 3:
The Great Plane Disaster

Location: Flight from London to New York

What happened: I was on my way to meet a friend for a week's holiday in New York and so was feeling glad to be alive and generally well disposed towards humanity. The person in the seat next to mine was a young bloke who seemed quite friendly, and I saw no reason why this shouldn't be a good flirting opportunity since we were never likely to meet again and it would help pass the time. Usually I just read or watch the film and don't get involved in conversations with anybody on planes, but this was the new me, the successful flirt. (Ha!)

I struck up a conversation by commenting on Brian's (well, you can't have everything) inability to open the in-flight peanuts, skilfully avoiding the potential pitfall of a hideously unfunny joke about nuts. He responded very warmly and we talked for an hour or so, during which I noted very positive body language. But after a while I realised that being strapped into a chair at 50,000 feet wasn't the best position to be in when you'd quite like to end a conversation with someone who seems increasingly over-eager. The flight was a nighttime one, and eventually I decided to tell Brian I was going to sleep for a few hours. I woke up and was rather alarmed to find I was being comprehensively groped. I was forced to slap him and, when that failed to have the desired effect, to call a steward.

Marks out of ten: Zero. (At least I didn't do anything terrible, though.)

Mitigating circumstances: The heady thrill of transatlantic travel?

The moral of the story: Never flirt with someone while travelling when part of the journey involves sleeping: at worst you'll be groped during your sleep, at best you'll wake up to find you've drooled all over yourself – and possibly your new friend.

Repercussions: None, but I was very quiet on the flight home.

How Not to Flirt 4:
An Angel at my Table

Location: Somewhere in Penge

What happened: A couple I know were giving a dinner party, I suspect because they'd been doing a lot of DIY on their recently acquired flat and were desperate for postive feedback. I arrived early owing to unexpectedly being able to follow the directions. While Dave and Caroline were having a starter-related disaster in the kitchen, I was ushered into the living room to find ... an Adonis sitting on the sofa.

I tried very hard to talk to Mr Beautiful

(it turned out he was Dave's brother), but sadly I was simply struck dumb by his gorgeousness. It was an hour before anyone else turned up, and during that time I managed to give a very good impression of a congenital idiot. Throughout the rest of the evening I reinforced the impression by a) communicating solely in monosyllables, b) spilling red wine over Mr Beautiful's dinner and c) uttering a small cry when I brushed his arm whilst reaching for the salt. I left as soon as I could, making a mental note never to socialise ever again.

Marks out of ten: Zero. (Again.)

Mitigating circumstances: It didn't help that the only single people there were Mr Beautiful and me, making me feel even more foolish.

The moral of the story: Obviously this was a flirting opportunity well and truly missed. I vowed never again to feel intimidated by someone else's good looks.

Repercussions: I no longer accept invitations to dinner, eating only at home alone.

How Not to Flirt 5:
Totally Inappropriately, at Work

Location: My office

What happened: I suspect it all started because I'd been thinking too much about handshakes. (It's at moments like this when I feel it's time to re-evaluate my life.) I was introduced to the new Vice Chancellor President Lord God Almighty bloke from the head office in Stuttgart, Herr Gruber, and immediately put out my hand to shake his (heeding advice on pages 81-84). I gave a nice firm handshake whilst looking him in the eye, and then – inexplicably – just gave a little squeeze, right at the end before letting go. I was horrified but I think I got away without showing it on my face. He looked startled.

I should explain that Herr Gruber is the most serious man I have ever met in my life. I didn't know that then, of course, but there were clues in his demeanour. He is so stiff that ... well, compared to him, the Queen looks like she's stoned. His watchwords are efficiency and excellence, and he has no time whatsoever for humour of any kind. I don't know if he has ever had a sexual relationship, but if he has I imagine it taking place only after the exchange of various forms in duplicate and the issue of an appropriate docket. From this point on he watched me with obvious suspicion and a stern countenance. Why, then, did I compound my error later on by winking at him in a suggestive fashion across the meeting room table, in full view of the managing director?

Marks out of ten: Minus twenty.

Mitigating circumstances: None that I can think of.

The moral of the story: It's possible to dwell too long on the handshaking advice on page 81.

Repercussions: I am now viewed with suspicion by the managing director as well, who undoubtedly sees me as a loose cannon. I no longer hold out even the remotest hope for any kind of promotion and am actively seeking alternative employment.

How Not to Flirt 6:
Get Horrendously Drunk Again

Location: The pub

What happened: I'm sure we've all been there – you go for a swift half after work and many hours later you're still in the pub, singing 'California Dreaming' and being restrained from standing on the table. However, it was what took place in the interim that constitutes my final flirting disaster:

A group of six of us arrived in the pub 'for a swift half' one Friday after work. Feeling inexplicably confident, I decided to try out the looking-then-looking-away technique (see page 76) on someone I liked the look of ... and it worked! My Flirtee came over and introduced himself, and we flirted (yes, I think I really can use the word) for a couple of hours. I even noticed postural echo (see page 93) at one point.

The effects of alcohol on an empty stomach are well documented and, unsurprisingly, I was legless by nine o'clock. I'm sure the poor man would have liked to get away before this, but I seem to remember that I'd pinned his arm to the table as I slurred my way through a long and drawn out account of my childhood (in the misguided belief that this was 'reciprocal disclosure' – page 113). The details are blurry, but I'm almost certain that at one point I removed my shoe and attempted footsie. Finally I came to my senses when one of my friends suggested we should leave, firmly clasping me by the arm and muttering an apology to the now broken man sitting beside me.

Marks out of ten: Four. (It started off well, at least.)

Mitigating circumstances: None.

The moral of the story: Again, I think it goes without saying that remaining reasonably sober is probably quite a good idea where flirting is concerned. Slurring, swaying and dribbling tend not to add to one's allure.

Repercussions: The search for a new job continues...

* * *

The above catalogue of disasters is a grim testament indeed. With a final score of minus five hundred million and fifteen out of ten, my only conclusion can be that I am a total and utter failure at flirting. Of course, the fact that I ignored all the advice has a lot to do with it. But perhaps, if I can overcome my tendency towards self-destruction, self-consciousness, lack of confidence and various obsessions, I'm not doomed to eternal failure?

I decided to find out how many other Flirting Failures were out there, and to what extent (and how) they were more successful than me...

FLIRTS OBSERVED

I knew I couldn't be the only failure around, and observing other people's flirting attempts seemed like a good idea at this point – maybe I'd end up feeling slightly better about my own dismal failure? So after an inevitable period of staying at home berating myself for my ineptitude, I put on a false nose and beard, unbolted the front door and ventured outside to observe other flirts.

Flirting Habitats

First of all, where do flirts go about their mysterious business? I turned to my pile of trusty flirting tomes where I discovered that the answer to this question is that they are, well, everywhere. One book listed over 70 different places where you could practise the fine art of flirting, from animal rights groups to zoos (honestly).

In a way, I had to agree – at least in theory – with the idea that flirting anywhere and everywhere is your best bet: it not only extends your flirting options but the people you choose to flirt with are probably going to be taken by surprise, which always makes them less defensive. Flirting seems so much easier when the focus is on something else.

Below are some of the places where I observed flirts in action – and in some cases, places where I had already attempted flirting myself. I've included my conclusions on the suitability of different venues for flirting of any kind, but in particular for the true flirting failure.

Internet chat rooms
Just say no, if you value your sanity. See page 35.

Supermarkets
I've never seen a singles night advertised at my local Sainsbury's, but I don't think there's any doubt that such things exist

unofficially. In fact it's probably just as well we don't have the official kind, since the very words 'singles night' represent the antithesis of true flirting. But supermarkets can be great places to flirt – and, as an added bonus, you get to have a nose at other people's shopping.

Meeting someone's eye over the tinned sardines may not be your idea of a romantic encounter. But if you consider what a welcome change it would be to have something other than brands of washing-powder to think about as you shop, you'll realise how open we all are to a bit of eye-eye. Research has shown that as people enter a supermarket, usually greeted by soothing displays of flowers and fresh veg, their heart rates drop and they fall into a suggestible, trance-like state that makes them highly susceptible to the wiles of the skilled flirt. However, heart rates soar in the queue for the check-out (due to the imminent prospect of having to pay for everything), so there's no point in flirting as you queue to pay – your fellow customers will be emerging from their trances and will by now be too alert to be fooled into flirting with you.

During the course of my own research I witnessed many flirtatious encounters in several leading supermarkets. However, a word of warning: keep away from melons and plums, as you may find the temptation to make some tragic innuendo simply too great. I overheard a truly excruciating exchange in the organic fruit and vegetable section: after exchanging a few words, two strangers (who obviously quite fancied one another) lapsed into silence. The obvious thing would have been to smile and head off to the ready-washed salads. But Mr Flirt was clearly not going to give up easily (making him Mr Not-very-good Flirt) and finally blurted out: 'Umm ... sorry ... I was just admiring your melons.'

Any shopping experience can be turned into flirting – keep your eyes open and your wits about you and you'll find that the queue for the deli counter need not be the dull experience it once was.

Restaurants

First, an unbreakable rule for all of us to bear in mind – never eat anything in what's supposed to be an erotic manner. We shall consider the hideous spectacle of the suggestive eating of a banana on page 91, but of course the same principle applies to all foodstuffs. In your imagination, it might well look attractive to nibble provocatively on an asparagus spear, licking your lips and fingers seductively (in the manner of Nigella Lawson). As I found during my research, the reality is quite different. Remember, there is nothing more off-putting than letting it appear that you're *trying* to look alluring: you will just look desperate and ridiculous.

In fact, restaurants don't make the best places to flirt, and not only because of the temptation to fellate crudités. This is because you will be unable to move around very much throughout the meal and therefore a) your choice of who to flirt with is limited, and b) once you've decided to flirt with someone, getting away is impossible until you leave the restaurant. These won't be particularly great hurdles for successful flirts: during three courses at the Thai Palace I witnessed one woman flirting with two waiters and all the people sitting at her own table (including me), as well as several other innocent bystanders. But Flirting Failures should be wary of this location.

Dinner parties

You've been asked to dinner, and the host mentioned a couple of other people who'd be going. But when you turn up you find that everyone else is in a couple apart from you and one other single person. (See also my own dinner party disaster on page 40.) It's almost impossible to flirt under these circumstances, either with the other single person or anyone else, mainly because you feel as though everyone's asking the question 'Will they fancy one another?' (and, to be fair, some of them are). You'd have to be extremely thick-skinned not to let that affect you. You'll both be on the defensive to the point where it will actually be difficult to be civil to one another for fear the other person thinks you had a hand in organising the whole situation.

As well as that horrifying possibility, see above under Restaurants. Plus you'll have to think of sincere-sounding things to say about the food.

Singles bars

Singles bars, or pubs and clubs that are well known for being pick-up joints, are definitely not flirting meccas. There's not necessarily anything wrong with them, though in my experience they tend to be pretty grim. But the Whiff of Desperation is definitely in the air, and anywhere that screams 'Come here to pick someone up!' isn't going to have subtlety as its strong suit.

Singles bars are likely places to find people who think they are flirting but aren't, mainly because everyone is eagerly anticipating unbridled sexual activity in the very near future as a result of any human contact they might make. I discovered this at first hand when I went along to one in the name of research. God, it was awful. While the friend I was with was in the toilet, a strange man sidled up to me and placed his hand firmly on my left buttock, looking shifty but un-apologetic. When I removed his hand no less firmly, he simply shuffled off, presumably to find out whether his charms would work on some other lucky woman. Now, you can't call that flirting, can you?

Evening classes

Do you honestly think people attend evening classes in order to learn something? Well, obviously some of them do, otherwise no one would acquire any conversational Spanish after the age of 16. But you'd be surprised at how many people go along to FE colleges after work under the guise of studying The Postmodern Novel, while in reality their interest in literature comes a poor second to their interest in meeting lots of people and flirting with some of them.

I first found this out from my friend Tom, who joined a class on Egyptology last September. When I told him I didn't know he was interested in ancient history, he replied, 'I'm not. I just joined to meet birds.' Having established that Tom was aware he was talking out loud, I realised what flirting hot-beds evening classes must be. The only flaw I could see in Tom's plan was that he was likely to become very bored during lessons. If he'd joined a class he was interested in, he'd at least have one thing in common with the other students. I think he just chose Egyptology because it sounded vaguely intellectual and involved mummies. As it turned out, Tom's plan wasn't a success: unsurprisingly, the other people on the course were quite keen on their chosen subject and soon discovered that Tom wasn't, which aroused their suspicions.

Clubs

Clubs are generally more suited to straightforward picking up without any of the niceties of good flirting. For a start you can't really talk, so you'll have to rely mainly on body language – which isn't that fascinating. For research purposes, I tried to hold a flirtatious conversation in a club, but it mostly consisted of 'What?' 'Sorry?' and 'Can you say that again?' and I soon abandoned the idea. On the same night, I witnessed the horrible spectacle of someone dancing supposedly seductively in a misguided flirting attempt. Can I just say: for the love of God, no!

Parties

Parties, of course, are made for flirting. Yet how often do people get it horribly wrong? (We've already seen my own cautionary tale on page 33.) Even if you know very few people, you must know at least someone, which serves as an introduction to everyone else (unless you've gate-crashed, in which case saying you know Dave is always a good bet, but you'll have to think on your feet and be prepared to get out fast if necessary). There's always plenty of alcohol about to loosen inhibitions (though beware of becoming unspeakably drunk – refer back to pages 33 and 42 if you need a stern reminder), and there are bound to be like-minded people there because of the friends you have in common.

The gym/swimming pool

Books on flirting quite often suggest the gym as a good place to flirt. I'm sorry, but personally I can't imagine anywhere worse. To flirt successfully you need to feel attractive – need I say more? The last time I went to the gym it was for something called 'precision cycling', which means cycling very fast until your head explodes. At the end of the lesson, I staggered off the machine terrified that I was going to chunder, and remained incapable of tying my own shoelaces, let alone flirting, for the next hour. Every flirting failure knows that the whole point of the gym is that you make no human contact with anyone whatsoever at any point. Otherwise it would be unbearable and no one would go, as everyone in their right mind knows. But after recent observational research I am forced to admit that, amazingly, some people do flirt in the gym. Obviously, gym flirting is restricted to those who feel they have achieved the peak of physical perfection and wear a lot of lycra.

As for the swimming pool – well, I can see that it might be marginally better, since the sweat factor is removed. However, far more naked flesh is exposed and very few people feel comfortable enough with the lack of clothing for flirtatious encounters with other, equally flabby, swimmers. Also, amphibious flirts should beware of strange people who lurk at swimming pools with the main intention of ogling – they may even try to cop a feel if you're not careful.

The pub

It very much depends what type of pub we're talking about, but let's assume we don't mean the kind where the main clientele are six old men who are suspicious of strangers. Other kinds of pub are normally good flirting venues, especially the area around the bar, where people are much more open to approach. But beware of woeful drunks, and of getting very drunk yourself. The worst example I've seen recently was a particularly woeful drunk who came over to where I was sitting with friends: he attempted to pull up a stool, but lost whatever vestiges of credibility he still had by falling flat on his back with legs in the air when he went to sit down.

Bar staff are, of course, notorious flirts, and I noted many of them flirting with customers during the course of my research. Not only are they singularly well placed for flirting (a huge turnover of potential Flirtees), but there's always a new conversational opener as people order the next round. The only drawback for bar staff is that it can be difficult to get away from unwanted attentions.

Work

Everyone knows that the coffee machine, the kitchen, the water cooler and similar areas of every office in the whole world are Designated Flirting Zones. Actually I needed quite a long time to work this out, but I always was a bit slow on the uptake. If you work in an office, it's a wonderful environment in which to flirt – flirting always feels more natural if there's an outside activity to focus on, and the work place provides this perfectly.

I've been on the look out for flirting in my own office, and have spotted several examples, from the board room to reception. There is nearly always someone in any office who has a reputation for being a flirt: in my own, this person is an idiot called Simon who is known to have shagged at least two other employees. I can find no real evidence whatsoever for Simon's mysterious success rate. And I certainly wouldn't describe him as a good flirt.

Be careful if a flirtation turns into going for secret drinks after work, progressing to hand-holding, and possibly a one-night stand or even a deep and meaningful relationship lasting several months or years. Office romances are notoriously difficult to maintain and without doubt you will be laughed at behind your backs by other members of staff. Keep in mind my own tragic attempt at office flirtation and beware of stiff international company presidents, if you value your career.

Plane/train journeys

These are great flirting opportunities, unless you happen to find yourself sitting next to a Mother Superior or a very deaf elderly man ... or indeed next to anyone you don't find attractive. But if you do find yourself next to someone fanciable (and on a train it's often fairly easy to arrange this for yourself), this is a great flirting situation. The excitement of travel on the Intercity Express (complete with stale sandwiches) makes everyone feel that little bit more adventurous, plus there is the added bonus of being almost completely sure that you will never see the person you're flirting with again – unless you specifically make arrangements to do so.

Meet the Flirts

The next stage of my extensive research involved meeting flirts (or people who thought they were flirts) of all types and in different situations. I was able to identify various different classifications – and it's interesting to note that both success and failure can sometimes fall within one type. These are the results of my careful interviewing (or earwigging, depending on the circumstances).

The Outrageous Flirt

This is the kind of flirt who will openly call himself or herself an 'outrageous flirt' or a 'terrible flirt' – and in some cases they are truly terrible. I found that the word 'outrageous' in this context often translates as 'obvious', and can denote use of sexual innuendo, as well as ridiculous physical 'techniques', such as gazing seductively from beneath lowered eyelids, or giving a slow wink. Although this type of flirt isn't going to win any prizes for subtlety, and wouldn't fit my definition of a good flirt, they can be successful with the young and naive.

The Flatterer
This type of so-called flirt needs no introduction. Some of them try extremely hard, it's true, and labour to come up with compliments you've never heard before ('your nostrils are perfectly symmetrical!'). One flatterer I met, who clearly saw himself as a bit of a ladies' man, would use the same opening line with any woman he'd met before – 'Have you lost weight?'. He did this without fail, presumably having read somewhere that it's the compliment women most like to hear. But he obviously didn't realise that, to be effective, you can only use it once or twice, most effectively when the woman actually has lost weight. Flattery is always completely transparent, and users of it are, without doubt, flirting failures.

The Comedian
These can be divided into two types – those who are genuinely funny and those

who are so toe-curlingly unfunny they make you wish you were at home defrosting the fridge. But even if they've just won the Perrier Prize, these people are often too self-centred to make really good flirts. They tend to be more interested in themselves and in showing off their Wildean wit than in the person they're trying to flirt with.

The Drunken Flirt

Getting very drunk before flirting is always a bad idea, yet many people persist – myself included. Drunken Flirts often assume that they've been flirting successfully, displaying their panache, wit and charm; whereas in reality this was only taking place inside their own heads. Alcohol-induced courage then inevitably leads the Drunken Flirt to do something ill-advised – for example, playing footsie under the table or clumsily grasping the other person's knee or hand. To illustrate this, here is a true story which provides a sobering lesson for us all.

A British ex-politician and famous lush

was at a diplomatic function in Peru. It was a free bar and as a result the politician was fantastically drunk when he spotted a vision in purple near the dance floor. Using all the charm at his disposal, he approached and, leering drunkenly, requested a dance. The reply he received was cutting: 'I won't dance with you for three reasons. First, you are drunk. Second, this is not dance music, it is the national anthem of Peru. And third, I am the Cardinal Archbishop of Lima.'

The Egomaniac

This is the type of pseudo-flirt most of us have come across at some point in the past. The Egomaniac will talk exclusively about himself or herself, and can sometimes overlap with The Comedian or Mr Double Entendre. Often this type of flirt fails utterly to find out anything about the person he or she is supposedly flirting with – happily delivering a monologue on his or her new car to a deep-sea-diving brain surgeon whose hobbies include juggling iguanas.

The Hard-to-get Flirt

You've probably noticed this kind of behaviour, or perhaps you've fallen victim to it: the Hard-to-get Flirt will charm expertly, giving the impression that he or she is really interested in the person s/he's talking to, then back off to the extent that the other person wonders if they've done something wrong. Given that flirting is all about both people concerned having a nice time, this behaviour definitely is not the mark of a genuine flirt. It's more the mark of a calculating, unpleasant manipulator. Sadly, it often works, and the victim ends up trailing around morosely after the Hard-to-get Flirt, desperate to get back into favour. If you're on the receiving end of this kind of behaviour, ask yourself why the Hard-to-get Flirt is doing it instead of wondering what's wrong with you. Either this person is very interested in you, or an attention-seeking maniac.

The Adolescent

You have to feel sorry for teenagers: all that angst, the raging hormones, the rampaging acne. Since they're new to the world of sexual attraction, pimply adolescents tend to be somewhat over-enthusiastic and clumsy, and very few of them manage anything that can really be thought of as flirting. Adolescent flirts are not necessarily aged under 18 – it seems that some of them just never grow up.

The Kindly Old Gent

It's funny, but I didn't think to include tea-dances in the above section on where to flirt. Yet that was where I found myself observing some interesting flirting behaviour. With a very few exceptions, everyone present was over 60 years old, and there were several old duffers whom I can only describe as excellent flirts. The Old Gents were impeccably polite, complimented the Old Ladies they flirted with and in general were totally charming. They obviously had a lovely time, and so did the women, some of whom flirted back very well too. I wondered if the OAPs were successful because the sexual element was so far in the background – could this be one of the secrets of being a good flirt? Or perhaps there were far fewer Flirting Failures in days gone by.

The Simperer

This throwback to a bygone era, almost exclusively female, will giggle coquettishly whenever an eligible man is within a five-metre radius, regress to a mental age of eight, and in extreme cases develop a lisp and an inability to pronounce the letter R. As if this wasn't ghastly enough, there may also be a certain amount of eyelash batting, gazing from beneath lowered lids (similar to the Outrageous Flirt, but worse), and pouting. Unbelievably, some men are charmed by the Simperer, but then there are a lot of people about who have mental health issues.

The Desperado

As we all know, there is nothing like the Whiff of Desperation to send potential flirts running for the hills. The Desperado need not be unattractive, dull or stupid (often the opposites are true): as long as he or she has an overwhelming desire to become part of a couple, any potential partner is guaranteed to be completely repelled. The sad thing is, Desperadoes often have the ability to charm people they're not attracted to, but with people they fancy they simply don't stand a chance. In some mysterious way they manage to communicate that, although this might seem like a casual conversation, in fact they are desperately looking for love and would like to get married and raise a family as soon as possible.

Mr or Ms Double Entendre

Find them in the supermarket enthusiastically and loudly pointing out juicy melons, or in restaurants nibbling breadsticks and remarking on their length and stiffness. The very worst offenders are the ones who try to pretend that they don't realise they're doing it, adding an appalling coyness to injury.

My final conclusion, having met a wide variety of different types of flirt, was that – as suspected – almost everyone is a Flirting Failure. Phew: I was not alone. Some types of so-called flirt are completely appalling, of course, while others are only slightly cringe-inducing. But very, very few are actually successful. People who aren't really aware of what they're doing are definitely the best flirts – many of them will deny that they flirt at all.

So, back to the start of my research, and the secrets of body language, conversation and confidence-building that I was desperately trying to put into practice...

THE BLACK ART
OF FLIRTING:
BODY LANGUAGE

Body language: subtle, enigmatic, mysterious. It was a complete mystery to a failure like me, anyway. As I began my research, I anticipated discovering little-known facts that would get results straight away – perhaps all good flirts knew that nose-scratching is a sign of hot-blooded desire, or that earlobe-touching indicates psychopathic tendencies?

It makes sense that body language is crucial to the way we communicate: we share more than 98 per cent of our DNA with chimpanzees, and it wasn't that long ago that we were all swinging through the trees and displaying our bums to each other by way of greeting, or sticking our toes up one another's noses as a sign of affection. So, during my research, it was no surprise to discover that any discussion of flirting puts lots of emphasis on the importance of non-verbal communication. I often came across the line that what we mean is conveyed 55 per cent by body language, 38 per cent by intonation, and only 7 per cent by what we actually say. I found out that these percentages refer to the 'emotional meaning' of a message, and that someone called Albert Mehrabian came up with them in the 1970s.

When you think about it, it's fairly obvious that a sentence can convey a variety of different emotional meanings depending on the way it's said, and with what accompanying body language. 'Nice to meet you,' could mean, 'You are a lowly worm and I am bored by the very thought of having to talk to you,' or, 'You look interesting,' or even, 'I am envisaging the two of us engaged in passionate sex.' It's true that body language and intonation are vitally important when meeting someone for the first time. The first thing you say to someone is likely to be completely bland, so the non-verbal clues will be almost all there is to go on.

Quite how Albert Mehrabian arrived at his very precise percentages is anybody's guess. It would be nice to think he just made them up and had a good laugh whenever someone mentioned them in a serious context. However, whether the percentages are particularly helpful or not, there's no doubt that body language is important. But now that we've evolved to the point where whooping wildly at mealtimes is no longer de rigueur, is it just too difficult to interpret body language accurately? Hopefully we'll have some conclusions by the end of this chapter.

Eye eye

Several hours into my research, I was heartily sick of reading about eyes being windows to the soul. Good grief. I was after hard facts – not bits of flowery vagueness – and eventually I did find a few. Of course, even I didn't need to be told that eyes are almost essential to communication. And it's easy to appreciate that eye contact is very powerful: just try looking into someone's eyes for more than three seconds – you'll find that it's almost impossible not to look away. (Tip: make sure it's someone you know and warn them first – unless of course you're in love, in which case make sure you do it somewhere private and give the rest of us a break.) And, of course, eye contact is crucial to flirting success...

The great thing about body language (or so I'd heard) is that you can use it to find out whether someone finds you attractive (and is therefore likely to want to flirt with you), without spelling it out in words, and so without risk of rejection and humiliation. I was dimly aware that one of the main ways of doing this was the whole looking-and-then-looking-away thing I'd heard about – but naturally, as a non-flirt, I'd never been able to understand it, let alone put it into practice. Now, however, I'm armed with the facts on this mysterious flirting technique (and have even managed to successfully use it):

A Failure's Guide to the Looking-and-then-looking-away Thing

1. Glance at the person you'd like to flirt with for just over a second then look away. It's important that your target (let's call him or her 'the Flirtee') catches you doing this, and that you look away just at the moment the Flirtee looks at you.

2. People can usually tell when they're being looked at, because in normal social situations people don't look into the eyes of anyone they don't know well, and if they do it's normally for less than a second. But if the Flirtee doesn't respond by glancing back at you, do it again.

3. If the Flirtee shoots a very quick glance in your direction then immediately looks away, it's likely that he or she knows you're looking and, frankly, wishes you'd stop. The target is almost certainly not interested.

4. Give it one more go to make sure.

5. On the other hand, if you and the Flirtee continue to cast surreptitious glances at one another, smiling when you catch each other doing it, it seems that – whey-hey! – you're in, and should feel free to go over and say something (we'll come to that minefield in the next chapter).

It seems so simple, doesn't it? And apparently it's hard to go wrong with this technique. However, it is possible to get the whole thing hopelessly wrong: in common with the rest of the animal kingdom, people find staring incredibly aggressive. So if you misjudge your timing you could end up making your Flirtee feel very uncomfortable or, at worst, violent. Make sure your glances last no more than a second and a half.

More eye-contact tips

My flirting studies further revealed the following pearls of wisdom:

★ It's vital to make *eye* contact straight away. Staring at your shoes and mumbling does not make a good impression, apparently. The eye contact should be direct and you should hold the other person's gaze as you say hello. If you don't do this, you will appear rude, or slightly shifty. I'm sure that even flirting failures will have grasped this point on their own, so we'll move swiftly along...

★ Because looking into someone's eyes can be hostile, *The Secrets of Allure* suggests that it's better to look at the general area of the face, letting your glance dart about 'playfully' (sorry). I would think this needs practice: you might end up giving the impression that there's a small fly buzzing around your Flirtee's head.

★ When you're talking to someone, you will naturally look away more when you're doing the talking; when the other person is talking, you should be looking at the other person's face for most of the time to show that you're listening. This all sounds pretty obvious, but some people do get it wrong: staring at someone unremittingly throughout the course of a conversation, or looking away when someone is talking to you will make the other person feel uncomfortable or unattended to. So if you get the feeling you're alienating people, have a think about this. However, I should add that if you're alienating everyone you talk to, also bear in mind that insults, arrogance, being really dull or threats of physical violence will also serve to alienate your new conversational partner. (See also the list on page 104.)

★ Dilated pupils indicate interest or arousal. (Or drugs.)

★ Worried that the person you're talking to is a pathological liar? It's quite hard to look someone directly in the eye when you're lying to them, so this could be something of a give-away.

However, the practised liar may have overcome this. Other signs are looking downwards, and 'eyelash flutter' (several rapid blinks, only lasting a fraction of a second).

★ Apparently we tend to blink more when we're attracted to someone, and that's why some women were in the habit of exaggeratedly batting their eyelids in the nineteenth-century American South and similar historical eras not famous for their subtlety. Thankfully those days are long gone and even *How to Titillate and Captivate* didn't recommend this. A woman batting her eyelids today would be assumed to have conjunctivitis.

Finally, I'd like to add a few of tips of my own, based on a lifetime's observations, before we move on from the subject of eye contact:

★ There is a difference between glancing flirtatiously and leering. Staring at someone's bum, especially accompanied by lewd shouts and hand gestures, is definitely leering.

★ It is very disconcerting for a woman to notice that the man she's talking to is in fact having a conversation with her breasts – and yet it's surprisingly common.

★ Don't you just hate it when people look you up and down, in that horrible sizing-you-up way? God it annoys me. Never do this. It is bad.

Outer Space

But eye contact isn't the only thing you have to think about. If, like me, you've never worried about invading anyone's personal space before, here's something new to nag away at the back of your mind...

Just like gorillas, chimps, baboons and other primates, humans are highly territorial. (Observe your boss when he comes back to his office to discover Brian from Accounts sitting at his desk: that 2 per cent of DNA really isn't very much, is it?) So the successful flirt is ever mindful of other people's personal space and always waits to be invited in rather than gate-crashing. Naturally, the personal space we are comfortable with varies according to the situation and other people involved – apparently, it's pretty specific:

0-45 cm Whispering, general canoodling, public transport during rush hour. Of course, this space is reserved for intimate relationships or, in the case of rush hour, total strangers with a variety of personal hygiene problems. Apart from the rush-hour example, when sadly no one has any choice in the matter, you would definitely need a very clear invitation before moving into this zone.

45cm-1.2m Casual conversations with people you know.

1.2-3m Conversations with acquaint-ances or people you've just met.

3m and over Talking to a group of people, maybe a meeting at work, or standing on a soap box at Hyde Park Corner offering advice on the dangers of peanuts, armchairs and anti-perspirants.

Surely, if people really did obey these rules of personal space, we'd all be shouting across one another in an effort to be heard, and quiet speakers would need megaphones to have conversations with people they'd just met. Perhaps the person who worked out these distances had an unfortunate groping experience at a formative age.

Then again, people invite one another to move closer in very subtle ways. Perhaps we're not happy when someone we know stands less than 45 cm away from us unless we've indicated that it's all right to be there – and people give and receive these messages without being aware of it. (45 cm does seem quite a lot to me, but it could be that I'm constantly offending people I know with my flagrant disregard of their personal space.) A person might invite you to come closer to them by...

★ smiling,

★ turning so that his/her body is facing yours,

★ leaning forward,

★ reaching towards you,

★ sweeping you into passionate embrace, or similar.

Conversely, you'll know you need to take a step or two back from someone when their body language shows they're not very comfortable, with gestures such as...

★ folding arms,

★ stepping back,

★ slapping you round the face,

★ holding up hands in guarded gesture,

★ shouting 'Get away from me!'.

It's definitely not a good idea to think too

long and hard about whether or not you're crossing uninvited into other people's personal space, as I realised when I found myself marking out 45 cm, 1.2m and 3m points around my desk at the office. But being aware that not everyone wants you to sit on their knee within the first five minutes of knowing them might not be such a bad thing.

How touching

Direct contact is even more problematic than personal space. There can be huge differences between how much touch different people think is acceptable, making things even more confusing. So how are we to negotiate this minefield?

Books on flirting tend to advise tactile people to curb their urge to touch just in case they cause offence. According to them, you should only touch someone you're flirting with on the arm, but absolutely never anywhere else. Hands are particularly sensitive and you definitely shouldn't touch someone's hand unless you know him or her well (apart from handshaking). But it occurs to me that this is rather a shame. If everyone followed this advice we'd all be stiffly avoiding any kind of contact with anyone who isn't a blood relative and worrying about whether we know someone well enough to ask them to pass the salt in case there's inadvertent finger brushing.

Personally, I don't think we need worry about this sort of stuff too much. As long as we don't actually grope anyone, there's enough for us to consider without this as well. If you naturally touch people a lot – great. Even if people don't particularly like it, it's unlikely that anyone would actually be offended. Apart from the Queen.

However, there are those who masquerade as naturally tactile people, while in reality they are *simply out to cop a feel*. Luckily these frauds are easy to spot: they are likely to touch other people as if by accident (though the law of averages tells you it has to be on purpose), they may hug people they barely know (and their hugs are often harder than necessary), they find they have to squeeze past people even though there's plenty of room to get by. In severe cases, finding a sweaty palm clamped to your thigh might not be out of the question. Fraudsters beware: we know who you are and we are not afraid to blow the whistle.

The handshake

This is often the first physical contact we have with someone else and, unless you're shouting gibberish or obscenities at the same time, the handshake can contribute a lot to first impressions. You might not have thought of shaking hands as a possible flirting technique, but, as we've already seen, flirting can occur in almost any situation, and one that begins with a handshake should definitely not be ruled out. Bear in mind that it was a purely innocent handshake that led to my work-related downfall on page 42.

I discovered that the most common complaint about handshakes is that they are either too weak or too strong – a weak handshake giving the impression of lack of confidence and general ineffectuality, whereas a strong one suggests aggression, or over-compensation for a lack of genuine confidence or a small penis.

The ideal handshake is nice and firm, without your hand lying limply in the other person's grasp like a halibut or, at the other extreme, painfully crushing the other person's fingers. Tips abound on types of handshake:

★ The 'glove' handshake, favoured by politicians, where you grasp the other person's hand with both of your own, using your left hand to cover the other person's right. This is in severe danger of seeming over-familiar and insincere when it's used on someone you've never met before – is it any wonder politicians are fond of it?

★ The 'left-handed brush' handshake involves all sorts of complicated stages, but basically you brush the other person's right hand with your left hand just after reaching out with your right hand. Confused? This one would have to be practised again and again with a very understanding friend – can it possibly be worth this investment of time, not to mention the strain on the friendship?

★ The 'fingers only', where you fail to grasp the other person's palm and end up holding just their fingers, is a type of handshake to be avoided at all costs. This is because if the handshake is firm you run the risk of crushing the fingers, and if it's weak the halibut impression will be even worse. Ensure palm-to-palm contact is made.

★ The Masonic handshake is a closely guarded secret ... until now. I can reveal that scratching your little finger three times across the other person's palm during a handshake will identify you as a member of a Masonic Lodge. Grand High Masters identify themselves with the little finger scratch while whistling 'The Laughing

Policeman'. Other signs include rolled-up trouser legs and obvious toupees.

★ The 'squeeze', involves giving the other person's hand a cheeky little squeeze at the end of the handshake, just before letting go, and which is supposed to be the most flirtatious type of handshake of all. (But see also page 42.)

The best handshake advice is probably simply this: look the other person in the eye; be the first to extend your hand; ensure that you make contact with the other person's palm and that your handshake is firm. Try the fancy stuff if you must, but you run the very real risk of everyone thinking you're a Mason.

Kissing hello and goodbye

The Flirting Failure will need no reminder that this is an area utterly fraught with misunderstanding and difficulty. When to do it? Which side should you lunge for first? Just one cheek or both? In extreme cases, confused and embarrassed kissers have been known to lose all sense of reason and deliver a prolonged full-frontal snog, causing a great deal more confusion and embarrassment to all concerned.

The only advice I have found to be of any use at all is this: take the initiative yourself, and either go in for a kiss (having decided on single or double beforehand – no last-minute veering) or hold out your hand to be shaken. Make absolutely sure you do not kiss with damp lips – this type of kissing should be moisture-free. Kissing someone hello when you've never met them before is unusual in Britain, though not unheard of, but when in doubt, shake hands.

Body Language No-nos

Never...

- ✗ try to flirt with food, for example eating a banana suggestively.
- ✗ snog someone you've never met before by way of greeting.

Do You Come Here Often?

✗ ask someone you fancy to see if there's something in your eye in pathetic attempt to lure him or her into close proximity.

✗ wring your hands cravenly.

✗ stare over the shoulder of the person speaking to you, or at the floor.

✗ enthusiastically hug everyone you're introduced to.

✗ cower.

✗ run your tongue over your top lip in the misguided belief that this looks erotic.

✗ touch your own or anyone else's primary or secondary sexual characteristics during flirting (obviously there are other times when this is OK).

✗ turn your back on the person you're talking to.

✗ on being introduced, accompany your handshake with a ribald wink.

Posture Pointers

The word 'posture' makes me think of 1950s debutantes wandering about with piles of books balanced on their heads under the stern gaze of a finishing school teacher. Whatever that was supposed to achieve – apart from looking ridiculous – I don't think it qualifies as a flirting tip. But the subject of posture does pop up in information about flirting, and apparently a lot can be read into the way and direction in which people carry themselves. You might have heard that if someone adjusts their position so that their body is directly facing yours, or their crossed leg is pointing in your direction, it's probably a sign that they're interested in you. Then again, it's probably a good idea to remember that it's very common to adjust your position to have a conversation with someone – and obviously not all conversations are flirtatious.

Apparently, the most positive body language of all is something known as 'postural echo', or 'mirroring'. This is when two people make the same actions at almost exactly the same time – reaching for a drink at just the same moment, crossing or un-crossing legs, both sitting in the same position – like a mirror image of one another. This behaviour is easy to spot and is an example of body language that, unus-ually, isn't open to different interpretations. If you notice it's happening to you (unlikely I know) try not to faint with surprise.

Many flirting books give the dangerous advice that it is a good idea consciously to mirror the person you are with, in order to make them feel more comfortable and positive towards you. Postural echo is not only an easily observable sign, the books argue, but can be artificially man-ufactured as a flirting tool. However, surely the odds must be stacked against anyone attempting this looking anything other than a complete fool. Be warned, and try this course of action at your own peril.

Do you speak ... body language?

We've barely skimmed the surface of the vast subject of body language here. There are countless aspects of non-verbal communication. Some of them are so familiar and easily interpreted that even failed flirts can be expected to know about them: smiling, yawning or running away, for example.

Find out if you can correctly translate the common non-verbal signals in this quiz...

1. Flared nostrils mean...
a) interest
b) funny smell
c) euphoria

2. If someone juts out their chin, it's a sign of...
a) madness
b) lust
c) superiority

3. You can tell if someone's smile is genuine by...
a) whether or not 'crows' feet' are formed near the eyes – if they are, the smile is genuine

b) whether or not the teeth are shown –
if they are, the smile is genuine
c) an accompanying round of applause

4. Widening of the eyes can denote...
a) tiredness or boredom
b) anger, surprise or fear
c) this person is utterly in your power

5. If a man's Adam's apple jumps up and down, it means...
a) he has something stuck in his gullet
b) he is sexually aroused
c) he is anxious, embarrassed, or
disagrees with you

6. A clenched jaw is a sign of...
a) a person who seldom changes their
socks
b) rage
c) depression

7. Touching or scratching the nose with finger and thumb can mean a person is...
a) lying
b) anally retentive
c) sincere

8. If someone exposes their inner wrists towards you, it's a sign that he/she...

a) has an Oedipus complex
b) feels threatened
c) likes and trusts you

9. Which of the following denotes attraction?

a) a curled lip
b) hair twirling
c) clenched buttocks

10. Inserting index finger into ear probably means the person is...

a) uncertain, anxious or fearful
b) relaxed and happy
c) attempting ear wax removal

Answers: 1a); 2c) (Interestingly, in Greece the chin jut means 'no', while in Ethiopia it means 'yes.'); **3a); 4b); 5c); 6b); 7a); 8c); 9b); 10c).**

Body language: a final thought

During the course of my research, I found several enthusiastic descriptions of rhythmic hand actions by women, particularly when 'stroking a cylindrical object' – body language which supposedly speaks volumes about 'what's really on her mind'. Pondering this over a drink in a pub, I realised to my utter horror that I do this all the time. My God – was I really obsessed by sex, even if subconsciously? Were people laughing at me behind my back for my transparent preoccupation with male genitalia? Surely, if I were genuinely thinking about penises all the time, the obsession would manifest itself in other ways? Was I some kind of repressed nymphomaniac?

Having calmed myself down with the aid of a strong sedative, I realised that, in all likelihood, my rhythmic hand movements were probably just a nervous habit devoid of sexual overtones. Possibly, though I'm not trying to cast aspersions, it would be nice for certain people to imagine that any woman stroking her wine glass is in reality inadvertantly advertising what she'd like to be doing to the sexual organs of any male in her vicinity. (I'd hate to destroy anyone's dreams totally: maybe some of them are.)

Given that it's easy to get it wrong, is body language really worth studying and worrying about? Eventually I came to the conclusion that it's interesting to be aware of it, but it's definitely not a good idea to become interested in it to the point of obsession – and any attempts at self-consciously altering your own body language should be made with the utmost caution. It is difficult to interpret, so if you notice someone's flared nostrils you shouldn't assume their owner finds you irresistible – maybe they've just got a troublesome bogey. If someone scratches their nose while speaking, they're not necessarily lying – perhaps they have an itchy nose. Notice different types of body language which all point to the same thing, and interpret them in addition to what a person is saying. But don't assume that one isolated action means someone is deeply bored, lusts after you or is a pathological liar.

If we were chimps, we'd read one another's body language accurately every time. We'd also have the joy of checking each other's body hair for lice on a daily basis and making sure the alpha male got the best bananas. But part of our evolution has been the development of sophisticated verbal language...

THE BLACK ART OF FLIRTING: CONVERSATION

As we noted earlier, whatever the importance to flirting of non-verbal communication, you can't just talk a load of old pants and expect people to be attracted to you for your stunning use of body language. However, most Flirting Failures bemoan never knowing the right thing to say, or how to start conversations with strangers. Heaving a troubled sigh, I forced myself to relive some of my own recent attempts. The worst examples fell into one of three categories:

★ Remaining mostly silent whilst being comprehensively bored by someone else.

★ Wittering desperately, aware that other

person may slump into coma at any time.

★ Periods of total silence punctuated by increasingly desperate conversational gambits from either party.

Of course, there's plenty of advice around, as I discovered during the course of my exhaustive research on the subject (which involved several actual conversations with real people). Putting my dismal track record behind me, I set out to discover the art of good conversation...

Opening-line angst

How do you start a conversation in the first place? It's not surprising that this is incredibly difficult for the true Failure: what is the point, when the ultimate outcome will be a terrible embarrassed silence broken only by the sound of tumbleweed sweeping past? Apparently, it's men who suffer most from opening-line angst. So it's really no wonder that it's usually men whose heads get turned by the dreadful allure of...

Chat-up lines

Face it: no one can get away with these. They're incredibly corny and, worse, they're an obvious sign of premeditation, which is horribly unappealing. Also, what they're saying is extremely clear: 'I am making a (very clumsy) pass at you' – which isn't terribly subtle. The most likely responses from a complete stranger are derisory laughter or horrified silence, during which the foolhardy deliverer of the chat-up line can only shuffle off in embarrassment (and serve him or her right, you might think). Chat-up lines should only ever be used as a joke, among understanding friends. Thinking about it – chat-up lines should *never* be used, even as a joke among understanding friends. You only need to look at a few to realise how terribly, utterly wrong they are...

Do You Come Here Often?

Hi, my name's Dave, but you can call me tonight!

Don't call us, mate, we'll call you.

If I said you had a beautiful body, would you hold it against me?

This line was immortalised in a 1970s song — it wasn't funny then and it isn't funny now.

Is there an airport nearby, or is it my heart taking off?

If someone says this to you and there IS an airport nearby, get on the first flight.

I hope you have a driving licence, because you're driving me crazy!

Rather than off the edge of a cliff?

> **Your eyes just told me everything except your name.**

Obviously, not quite everything.

> **'Is it hot in here, or is it you?'**

Clearly it isn't you.

> **Do you believe in love at first sight? Or shall I walk past again?**

I think we've suffered enough – the point's been made, hasn't it?

Now we've established that chat-up lines are a very bad idea indeed, what *is* a good opening line? You might groan, as I did, at the answer to this given by every book on flirting ever written: it doesn't matter what you say, it can be any old twaddle – the point is to say something.

Anyone who isn't a total horror or a tosser of the highest order will respond to any verbal overture and say something in reply. There are very few people rude enough to blank you completely – so take heart. Spending ages thinking of something witty or clever to say won't help you very much: it won't sound as though you've just thought of it (purely because you haven't), and to flirt effectively you need to be spontaneous. However thrillingly insightful your carefully prepared comment might be, it could end up having almost as bad an effect as a tragic chat-up line due to its lack of spontaneity. When you think about it, the opening line is simply asking, 'Is it OK to talk to you?' If the response is positive ... well, that's where the trouble really starts.

However, I'd advise *against* coming out with the first thing you think of to say. The following, to give a few examples, should never be used as opening lines – if one of them pops into your head spontaneously, never say it out loud:

★ 'Is that a boil?'

★ 'Please talk to me. I'm begging you.'

★ 'Horizontal stripes with an arse like that? Are you mad?'

★ 'Did you smell that? It wasn't you, was it?'

★ 'I collect spoons.'

★ 'It's true there are better looking women here, but there's something about you that just seems really interesting.'

★ 'God, I'm bored.'

★ 'So. You're not talking to anyone either.'

★ 'That's not contagious, is it?'

Assuming that you've said something as an opener that didn't result in a slap or a horrified silence, but in some kind of reply or encouraging smile from the other person, what is the next step for the Flirting Failure? In my experience, it is to cast desperately about for conversational gambits, blurt out some piece of old nonsense, and then face the inevitable slide into staring at your shoes unable to think of anything to say, until eventually one of you finds an excuse to leave. How are we to avoid this excruciating situation?

Beyond the opening line

Of course, there's no foolproof way to make sure your conversation doesn't turn into a hideous toe-curling nightmare. But I did manage to find some tips on how to lessen the risks.

Firstly, it helps to remember that everyone likes talking about themselves, or about subjects close to their heart, whether it's synchronised swimming, politics or their budgie. And when people start on a subject they feel passionately about, what they say is likely to be interesting (unless it's dull, offensive or idiotic, of course). It's easy to say that some people are just unbelievably boring and need to be avoided at all costs. However, someone with a more sunny disposition might say that everyone has the ability to be entertaining, the trick is to discover how to bring that out.* Perhaps this is the real secret of being a successful flirt?

My research material heartily recommended active listening as the single thing most likely to turn Mr Loft Conversion into Oscar Wilde. This means concentrating hard on what the other person is saying, avoiding distractions, and remembering to button your lip no matter how tempting it is to interrupt and pipe up with some hilariously and marvellously witty story of your own. This is more difficult than it sounds. Very often, people listen to a conversational partner with only a small proportion of the brain, enabling them to give the impression that they're taking in everything the other person is saying. In fact, the rest of the brain is actively engaged in mentally compiling a shopping list, thinking about sex, or formulating the next thrilling instalment of their own monologue.

* In the interests of healthy cynicism, the author wishes to assert the existence of crashing bores in all walks of life, and does not advise spending too long in trying to find out whether such people have hidden depths beneath their dull exteriors.

What the average brain is thinking about during conversation:

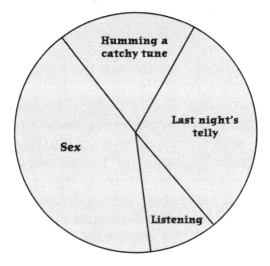

Many of us Flirting Failures spend a lot of time worrying about how we can amaze and delight everyone we talk to with our fascinating anecdotes and witty repartee, when we'd be better off just listening carefully. The chances are that you'll get a lot more out of the conversation, and at the same time completely charm the person you're talking to. You could even say you'd be flirting successfully.

However, before we all float away on a fluffy cloud of happiness where everyone is fascinating and full of love for everyone else, a small word of caution: someone who is prepared to blether on about themselves in answer to your astute and insightful questioning without asking you anything in return is possibly not the most sensitive person in the world. Are you sure this is someone you want to flirt with? Generally speaking, we Flirting Failures tend to get things wrong by worrying so much about being witty that we don't listen, and get stuck for things to say. But beware of talking to egomaniacs – a bit of give and take is necessary.

Some areas to avoid

Perhaps it's a good idea to remind ourselves at this point that there are some areas we'd all be well advised to steer clear of in first conversations:

★ The time you became obsessed by someone to the point where they claimed you were stalking them.

★ Sexual fetishes.

★ The various levels of a computer game, in exhaustive detail.

★ Obsessive loathing for boss/ neighbour/people chosen at random.

★ The fact that you have fat thighs/don't like your nostrils/wish you had straight hair.

★ Your tendency to get cystitis at times of stress ...

★ ... or any minor ailment – you're not 85 yet.

★ Your long and comprehensive criminal record.

★ Any minority hobby or interest of yours, unless the other person has specifically asked about it – eg malt whisky, pit bull terriers, rubber wear or wooden spoons.

★ The type of man or woman you're most attracted to – this will not fail to make someone feel unattractive, ill at ease and inadequate, unless it describes him or her in intimate detail, which is not recommended either.

Reciprocal disclosure

Aren't scientific terms like this great? This is one of my favourites (along with 'postural echo'). It means disclosing personal information to the person you're flirting with and having them reciprocate by telling you something about themselves. You might think that this must mean very personal information, like whether or not you received enough emotional support from your last long-term partner, or how old you were when you lost your virginity. In fact, rather disappointingly, it just means any information about yourself. When you've just met the person you're flirting with, this type of information can be as trivial as whether or not you like ice-cream or whereabouts you live. If both people reveal a roughly equal amount about themselves during a conversation, apparently it means that they are getting on very well. And it goes without saying that the more personal the information, the better.

However, this can be difficult to judge: you've said you don't like sprouts, but she's expressed a preference for the Algarve over the Costa del Sol – who's disclosed the most? The Flirting Failure might well get caught up in such a mental dilemma and completely miss the fact that neither of you have said anything at all for the last five minutes. Remember that, along with body language, this kind of thing is interesting to note, but beware of becoming obsessed by it.

Positive and negative

Just about every piece of material on flirting I've dug up during my extensive research carries the advice that you should never be negative. Negativity is, apparently, the kiss of death and you will be universally shunned if you voice anything other than cheery thoughts. We are warned that just one chance remark about global warming in an unguarded moment could spell social suicide.

Of course, this is not all complete nonsense (note positivity here). If someone announces they're going on a diving holiday, they're not going to be best pleased if you respond by saying, 'But have you considered the risks? Good god, man, the bends is one of the most painful ways to die imaginable!' The type of person who always manages to see a bad side to any given situation is clearly not going to be surrounded by swarms of admiring fans. (Could this be why you're a Flirting Failure? How many times do you begin a sentence with 'Oh no!' 'That's terrible!' or, 'I don't mean to depress you, but...'?)

However, you can go to extremes in the opposite direction. One of the many books I read as research gives this example: you are told by a stranger of his plan to start a business exporting ice to the Arctic, or something equally ill-advised. Apparently, you would be making a big mistake if you were to respond by pointing out the lack of wisdom inherent in the stranger's scheme: this would definitely not be good flirting. Oh no. According to *The Secrets of Allure* (good grief), your response should be along the lines of, 'Wow! Ice to the Arctic, eh? There's something I'd never have thought of!' But surely, the reason you'd never have thought of it is because you're not completely out of your mind. If this is one of the secrets of allure, maybe only idiots are alluring. Why on earth would you want to flirt with someone who is both stupid and determined to bankrupt himself? Tell him he's bonkers and hopefully he'll keep his hare-brained schemes to himself.

After careful consideration, my advice would be this: be as negative as you like if that's how you feel about something, as long as you don't actually insult anybody, and as long as you're not negative about a lot of things a lot of the time. Nobody likes someone who's constantly moaning, but equally irritating are people who skip about looking for the positive in every situation no matter how terrible. And there are worse things in life than being thought of as an embittered old trout.

The Conversational Crutch

Just about everywhere you look for flirting advice you'll find the tip that all good flirts should carry something interesting or unusual with them. The idea is that the item becomes a conversation piece, so it has to be something you can tell a story about. (It would be a bad idea to wander about with a large framed photograph of a hamster and not to be able to give a reason for it when questioned.)

This might sound like the silliest piece of advice imaginable, but if you do ever try going to the pub carrying a pot plant or a small chest of drawers you'll find that a lot more people speak to you than usual – which is good because it solves the problem of opening-line angst. On the other hand, it means that you're not the one who chooses the people you want to speak to – they choose you – though it's easy to give a dismissive answer to their opening questions that gently makes it clear further discussion is not welcome.

However, I don't know about you, but there's something about the whole idea that makes me a bit uneasy. Either you'd have to have a genuine reason for carrying your item (which limits what it could be) or you'd have to make something up which sounded totally convincing. If anyone suspected you'd brought your item along purely so people would talk to you, they'd run a mile ... as well they might.

I came to the conclusion that the unusual item gambit has the Whiff of Desperation about it and should be avoided. Of course, if you do ever find yourself in the enviable position of having to meet your friends after work with a pot-bellied pig tethered to your arm (or similar), prepare for an evening as a flirting success.

Compliments

How could any book with the word 'flirting' in its title get by without mentioning compliments? Most of us are a writhing mass of insecurities and therefore we love a compliment, so a good flirt will be adept at using them. But how do you deliver them and not sound lame or insincere, oily or ingratiating?

Again, my trusty pile of flirting books came into their own on this subject. Their advice is that you should always compliment sincerely – which sounds reasonable, we can all sniff out flattery a mile off. Secondly, compliments are much more effective when they are specific – so 'that colour suits you' is better than 'you look nice'. If you think about it, you'll probably find that the compliments you've received in the past that stick in your memory are the more specific ones – you can remember who gave them and when and where – whereas you probably don't remember the times people have said you looked nice, or vaguely that you made a good job of something. Finally, try to think of something unusual to compliment somebody on, rather than the obvious, as again it'll be more likely to stick in the person's mind.

All of this advice sounds fair enough. Let's have a look at some of the books' examples:

'Mary, the compassion you show towards others has truly inspired me.'

'Karen, the kindness and support you have shown makes you a very special person.'

'Joe, you are such a motivational person due to your inner energy and enthusiasm.'

'Brian, have you been to a health spa? Your skin is truly glowing.'

'Patricia, the dark grey of your new suit contrasts well with your hair colour and makes you look professional and dynamic.'

It's actually quite embarrassing just to read these lines in the privacy of your own home, let alone utter them aloud to another person, isn't it? It makes you wonder if it's possible to cringe to death. Suddenly 'You look nice,' sounds really good. So perhaps we should add an extra piece of advice on the giving of compliments: never give a compliment that oozes oil and sounds as though it took you some time to compose it in your head – it will be buttock-clenchingly embarrassing for all concerned.

On the other hand, it might be that someone compliments you. Having thought about compliments I've received in the past and how I've responded to them, I've decided that the best advice is this: whatever you're being complimented on, say thanks and then shut up. You might be tempted to give a little talk about the particular area of excellence in question: resist it. Much more likely for a failed flirt, you might feel that you should refute the compliment: this is just as bad. Just accept it and pipe down. The last time someone told me I looked nice, I said something along the lines of 'What? No I don't – my arse looks enormous and don't tell me you haven't noticed this huge spot!' Yes, I truly am a Flirting Failure.

If you get an overwhelming urge to protest when someone compliments you, it could be that, like me, you have an in-built compliment translator. For example:

Compliment: Your hair/whatever looks nice.

Translation: Normally it looks terrible.

Compliment: You look healthy.

Translation: Christ, have you put on two stone since I last saw you?

Compliment: Have you lost weight?

Translation: You look pallid and sickly.

Compliment: My god, that was fantastic!

Translation: I've had better, love.

Compliment: You're a good driver.

Translation: I'm telling you this in an effort to keep everyone calm and avoid screaming in panic.

Compliment: You work well under pressure.

Translation: You couldn't give a stuff about anything, could you?

You Bein' Funny?

It's difficult to think of a flirtatious conversation that's totally serious, and because of this all of the flirting books I've come across have a little section on humour. As you can imagine, though, it's even more difficult to give advice on this than on conversations in general. Which probably accounts for the earnest manner in which the books talk about being humorous. But you could be talking about something quite serious, or at least ostensibly serious, and still be flirting quite successfully. Just because both of you aren't doubled up with laughter every couple of minutes it doesn't mean things aren't going well.

A word of warning here: the chances are, when you're talking to someone you don't know very well, if you decide to tell a rehearsed joke (such as 'did you hear the one about the horse who goes into a pub...'), it will go down like a lead balloon. Generally speaking, premeditated humour is ... well, just not funny.

The end

Inevitably, there will come a point when the conversation has to end. You might decide that the person you're talking to is a tosser of the highest order and that you must make your escape before you are forced to kill him. Or it might be that you have just enjoyed a fascinating conversation and want to quit while you're ahead. Sometimes this will happen without you having to do anything at all – you might be interrupted by a third person, the person you're talking to might end the conversation for you, or possibly an event (such as earthquake, illness or injury) might force you to abandon your chat.

Quitting while you're ahead is a very good idea because it will leave the other person wanting more. If you wait for the conversation to falter you're not going to leave the other person with the best impression: the image of you standing there silently with a fixed grin on your face for what seems like several millennia is not likely to make a happy memory.

Flirting Failures know only too well the terrible feeling of being unable to get out of a conversation that is beginning to flag (or that flagged some time ago and is now dying a slow and painful death), or the no less terrible situation of ending up in a corner with someone offensive or boring. (There are some people who will not be distracted from the subject of house prices in Manchester no matter what, and we'll assume that you've done your best.)

Next time you find yourself stuck, first of all make sure you say how much you've liked talking to them before you make your excuse – if possible personalise this somehow (e.g. 'I'll remember what you said about finger buffets!'). Then try one of the following, depending on the situation...

★ You can just say you've got to go without sounding rude, as long as you say you've enjoyed the conversation.

★ If you're anywhere there are people you know, say you need to speak to/find someone.

★ If there are people you know within arm's reach, bring them into the conversation.

★ Express a hope that you'll see the other person later on, and with luck they'll take it as a cue.

★ Say you're off to get a drink/some food.

If you've been talking to an absolute tosser and want to offend him/her, try the following:

★ Shout, 'Look over there!' Now run away.

★ Go to sleep.

★ Say, 'See ya – wouldn't want to be ya!' as you beat hasty retreat.

★ Yawn long and loudly, shake head, leave without further explanation.

★ Ask, 'God, is that the time?' when you are plainly not in vicinity of watch/clock.

★ Assume glazed expression; start backing away.

Well, I'm sure you're now desperate to go out and strike up a conversation with a total stranger. In fact, it's not surprising that conversations with strangers can hold so much terror for the Flirting Failure – part of the reason we're not successful flirts is that we're a bundle of insecurities, which we'll be picking over in the next chapter...

THE CONFIDENCE TRICK

So we've studied some of the mysteries of body language and conversation and now know all about postural echo, personal space and some truly appalling chat-up lines. But as most Flirting Failures are all too painfully aware, confidence is the true key to successful flirting. Tips are all very well, but nothing's going to turn you into a good flirt if you're riddled with self-doubt and feel too shy to put any of that advice into practice.

Flirting is all about two people telling one another how attractive they are – it acknowledges the fact that attraction is in the air, even though it's not even remotely serious. You can't acknowledge someone else's interest in you unless you're confident about yourself.

Before we go any further, let's have a look at the dread subject of appearance, since it's so bound up with how we feel about ourselves...

Looks are everything

It's very easy for most of us to think we're less than gorgeous. You can't turn round without some aspect of the media making you feel you're too fat with short legs, or that you have too many wrinkles, too much cellulite and not enough cheek bone. Maybe things would have been easier a hundred or so years ago – but then again, washing-machines, penicillin and computers do come in quite handy, so maybe not. Living in the twenty-first century has a lot to recommend it, but it's fair to say that this is an age obsessed with appearances. It's not difficult to become over-critical and under-confident about how we look, and this is increasingly true of men as well as women. Even Raving Beauties moan about the size of their thighs, or the little mark behind their ear that's a chicken-pox scar but you can really see it in bright daylight if you use a magnifying glass ... and bloody irritating they are too.

Maybe the first thing to bear in mind is that, obviously, how attractive we are does not solely depend on the way we look. Imagine a fantastic looking man. We'll pause here a moment to admire his physical perfection from every angle. Now imagine him saying, 'Oi, you. Get your coat, you've pulled.' OK, you might need to imagine him picking his nose and saying he enjoys torturing kittens as well. Now imagine him saying it in the voice of David Beckham. See what I mean? Conversely, you can be devastatingly attractive without necessarily being conventionally 'beautiful' or 'handsome' (and what these things mean varies according to fashion and culture anyway).

Secondly, we are all different shapes and sizes. Anything or anyone that says all women should be a size eight, or all men be toned and muscular, should be viewed with utter contempt. You might as well say all men should be six foot four with dark hair, or all cats should be black and white. One of my dodgily titled research books (*How to Titillate and Captivate!* this time) even offered the advice 'Be slim!' as one of its top ten flirting tips. Good grief, this is all we need. Being a successful flirt has nothing whatsoever to do with your inside leg measurement or the size of your bum.

So now that I've cleared that up, we can all stop worrying about how we look, can't we? Of course, this is almost certainly not going to happen. The likelihood is that some days we'll feel attractive and some days we'll think we look like bog monsters. But if we all make a concerted effort not to focus on the size of our noses, our cellulite or encroaching baldness, the world will be a much happier place and a lot more flirting will go on.

I Haven't Got a Thing to Wear

While we're on the subject of appearance, it goes without saying that you should wear whatever you feel comfortable in and roll your eyes in a bored sort of way if the fashion police try to arrest you. Or you would think it goes without saying. *How to Titillate and Captivate!* shares these invaluable tips:

★ Men look good in jackets with patches on the elbows, in style of maths teachers of yesteryear.

★ Grey and maroon are both unattractive colours for any woman to wear.

★ Men think that women who wear jewellery are cheap.

★ Wearing too much brown and black makes men unattractive.

★ Women should wear thick woollen scarves in winter because it will make men think of cavorting in the snow with them.

Well, I'm sure we've all learned something useful there. In fact, there are only five ways you can dress for a definite lack of success...

★ Wear socks with sandals.

★ Wear one of those nylon slips and make sure it's visible below the hemline of your skirt.

★ Wear a toupee, or indeed do anything at all to try and disguise the fact that you're going a bit thin.

★ Sport a wet patch on your trousers on returning from the loo (known in some quarters as 'a Wembley'), or in fact any stained clothing.

★ Go out in nightwear (unless in case of fire or similar).

Confident?

Now that we're all wildly happy about our looks and clothes, all we've got left to worry about are our individual psyches – nothing a few years of intensive psychoanalysis can't sort out, in most cases. But assuming we don't have several years and many thousands of pounds to spend working out why we're only attracted to short, bearded Germans (I can only speak for myself here, obviously), is there a quicker way of increasing our confidence and thus become successful flirts?

Well ... I hesitate to hold myself up as an example to Flirting Failures everywhere, but this is something I've tried that really works. It sounds simple, but don't let that put you off: if you don't feel confident, acting as though you do will make everyone else think you're confident ... and gradually you'll find that you *are* feeling more confident. It's really not very difficult to do this solely using body language – look people in the eye, don't stare at the floor or slouch (but make sure your posture isn't unnaturally rigid either), don't cover your mouth when you speak, be the first to extend your hand to shake the other person's (if it's that sort of do), and smile. You're probably thinking that this sounds like fair old rubbish, but give it a try and I'd be very surprised if you don't feel more confident simply as a result of being aware of your body language. I tried it when I started a new job a few years ago. Although I felt intimidated, I succeeded in fooling everyone into thinking I was an assertive, devil-may-care, no-nonsense type of person by carrying myself confidently, making eye contact and smiling gamely. Of course, it wasn't long before they discovered the truth, but even so.

There's no shortage of books that will tell you to go and stand in front of the mirror and repeat a little confidence-building mantra three times a day. Something along the lines of, 'I am a unique human being with special qualities to offer. These include kindness, intelligence, humour, patience and being good at cross-stitch' or some such old twaddle – obviously you have to fill in your own, *unique* qualities yourself. Personally I'd feel like a complete idiot doing that three times a day and I'd end up adding 'sad enough to stand in front of mirror telling myself I'm great' to my long and comprehensive list of failings.

The truth is, there isn't a single one of

us who doesn't have a little negative voice constantly nattering away along the lines of 'that hairstyle doesn't suit you god your backside is enormous why did you just say that you sounded like a cretin for christ's sake could you be any more of an idiot?' Or is that just me? No, it's OK, I've asked around and 98 per cent of the population of the whole world agrees with me. Some people are just better at appearing to be confident than others. Of course, there's the other two per cent who really are supremely confident because they just think they're great. What they don't know is that they're actually completely insufferable and no one really likes them.

How Not to Feel Confident

✗ Tell anyone who will listen how useless you are.

✗ Take a photograph of the thing you like least about your appearance, magnify it and carry it around with you everywhere. Look at it frequently to remind yourself how physically repulsive you are.

✘ Keep a mental list of your most embarrassing moments and refer to it whenever you catch yourself feeling happy.

✘ Keep a similar list of the times you've been rejected.

✘ Wear ill-fitting clothes you don't like.

✘ Assume that everyone else is more attractive, efficient, talented and likeable than you are – it's probably true.

✘ Try to have at least one example of your general uselessness at the forefront of your mind at all times.

Every one of us is a bundle of insecurities desperately hoping that no one will notice our obvious weaknesses and failings. (And if that doesn't make you feel glad to be alive, I don't know what will.) The reason most of us worry so much is because we want everyone to like us. But of course not everyone is going to like you – and, very often, nor would you want them to, when you really think about it. First of all, there's the Insufferable Two Per Cent who think they're great and whom everyone else actively dislikes (though often secretly). Would you honestly care if one of these egomaniacs disliked you as much as you do them? Then there are all the people with whom you just don't have much in common, or whose opinions you don't agree with – you don't necessarily dislike them, you just don't really care one way or the other. So why should you be bothered if you're not on their Christmas card lists? One of the keys to being a successful flirt is being interested in other people – but that doesn't mean you have to want them to like you. Caring too much what people think of you can have a lot to do with lack of confidence.

Well, we've come a long way since we first embarked on our journey to Planet Flirt. On the way we've heard plenty of tips –

some of them interesting, some of them useful, some of them very strange indeed which we'll try to forget about. We've also witnessed many flirting attempts by Flirting Failures (some of them – possibly the most tragic of all – my own). It's time to move on to the possible effects of flirting, successful or otherwise...

REPERCUSSIONS

If you've taken heed of the warning on page 22, you won't have an ulterior motive when attempting to flirt. However, whether you've failed or succeeded, you might well find that there are repercussions...

What Happens if I Pull?

Judging from pages 32–47 of this book, this is never likely to happen to *me*, I'll admit. (Or if it does, it certainly won't be as a result of my flirting techniques.) And of course this is not the object of the exercise. But since it's a possible – even if fantastically unlikely – outcome of flirting, I think we should be prepared.

1. The first thing to do is remain calm. Do

not say or do anything that indicates disbelief. This is the kind of thing that happens to you all the time!

2. Decide what your own intentions are. Do you like this person enough to spend more time with them, either on a date (which could be the first of many) or during a one-night stand? (Though see the next page for disadvantages of one-night stands.)

3. Determine your flirting partner's intentions. Are they the same as yours, or will you heartlessly crush their hopes and dreams? Or vice versa?

4. Proceed with caution. Though this advice will be rendered totally meaningless if you are drunk.

Now on to a far more likely scenario...

Rejection

First of all, here's something you probably weren't expecting (if you're a

The Disadvantages of the One-night Stand

• How do you know this person isn't going to hack you to death with an axe or poison you with contents of a sinister phial? This will inevitably play on your mind.

• You are probably drunk. This will lead to:
1. disappointing sex.
2. a hangover, compounding the general depression/disappointment/ self-loathing/disgust (delete as appropriate) of the next day.

In addition, you might wake up next to someone you wouldn't have gone near if you'd been sober.

• Are you sure this person isn't related to you in some way? This will also play on your mind.

• You will be faced with problematic leave-taking the next day.

true Failure, that is): what if it's *you* doing the rejecting?

How to get away from an undesirable type

The list of undesirable types is extensive – the one on page 8 is merely scratching the surface. Here, finally, is your guide to getting away from them...

★ Try one of the polite conversation endings on page 115.

★ Try one of the offensive conversation endings on page 116.

★ Pretend to faint.

★ Explain why you need to get away from him/her (eg she's boring you rigid/he's a sexist reptile).

★ Say you smell smoke or gas and rush off to ascertain the possible cause.

★ Try beating them at their own game –

she's giving you a blow-by-blow account of her loft conversion? Interrupt and tell her about the fluctuation in house prices in your area over the last five years.

★ Have a pre-arranged signal with a friend, such as scratching your ear or picking your nose. At the signal your friend comes over and tells you you're urgently needed elsewhere.

★ Place head in hands. Begin to rock slowly back and forth.

★ Simply run away screaming.

Books on flirting will tell you that you shouldn't be rude to anyone under any circumstances, as this is something a good flirt would never do. Well, I might be a Flirting Failure, but I think that's complete rubbish. Some people deserve a bit of rudeness – though I'll admit they're quite rare. But if someone's an appalling bigot, I think they should be told.

If you don't want to offend someone, it's

true that it can be difficult to get away. But it's essential that you do, for your own sanity.

Coping with rejection

It happens to us all. (Well, it probably happens to me more than most.) None of us is immune to the cold shoulder, and being spurned can be a truly horrible experience. To be cast aside, discarded like a worthless object ... Oh, for goodness' sake. The important thing to try to remember is that we're talking about flirting here, not proposals of marriage. And if you go all the way back to page 23, you'll remember that flirting is not a serious activity and there shouldn't be a purpose behind it. (If there is then it's not really flirting.)

As we found out in chapter four, there are ways to tell if someone's likely to be interested in you before you actually say anything, so being rejected shouldn't be an issue very often. But there's always going to be the odd time when you're made to feel unwelcome. As long as you really haven't invested anything in the encounter, so what? It shouldn't matter to you any more than any other random act of rudeness, and god knows you should be used to those by now.

But if you must insist on getting upset about it, here are a few tips on how to make yourself feel better...

★ If someone's been rude when rejecting you, this gives you the chance to be really rude back and feel totally justified about it.

★ You now have an excuse to gorge yourself on chocolate/large cake/use up a whole week's allowance of alcohol units in one night.

★ The person who rejected you probably did so because they're just generally horrible to everyone, not because of anything to do with you.

★ There's no need to make someone feel

rejected: this person obviously has no social skills whatsoever.

★ The person who rejected you is probably the sort who owns lots of soft toys and talks about them as though they were real people, or is insufferable in some other way. The people they are interested in are undoubtedly tossers of the highest order.

On the other hand, you could...

★ Make a list of your failings and wonder which of them was most responsible for the rejection.

★ Spend several days, or even weeks, weeping.

★ Punish yourself by doing something you don't like – rent a video of a film you hate, or offer to do someone's ironing free of charge for a month.

★ Take a look at yourself in the mirror:

are you honestly surprised you've been rejected?

★ Resolve never to try flirting ever again.

THE HALF-BAKED CONCLUSIONS OF A FAILED FLIRT

Well, it's nearly the end of the book. We've come a long way from when we first asked the questions, What is flirting? How is it done? And can I do it? And we've struggled towards coming up with some answers – in the case of the last question, we were able to arrive at a definite 'NO.' So what have we learned? Let's have a recap...

Those Half-baked Conclusions in Full

1. Make sure you're brimming with confidence – but probably best not to do this by repeating a mantra in front of a mirror, which will only make you feel like an idiot.

2. Don't become totally obsessed by body language and end up silently staring at people looking creepy and strange.

3. Smile (first ensuring no spinach or similar stuck in teeth).

4. Never eat or dance in what is supposed to be a seductive manner.

5. Don't think up something to say as an opening line and then deliver it word for word – premediation is not attractive.

6. Don't moan about the size of your bum.

7. Before you go anywhere, check clothing for suspicious stains, ensure you aren't wearing your pyjamas, etc.

8. Never French kiss anyone by way of introduction.

9. Chat-up lines are always a bad idea.

10. Never play footsie.

11. Never simper.

12. We should all get out more.

13. If you are secretly looking for love/ sex/a lift home/a pay rise/etc, you are not really flirting – it's not a means to an end.

14. Make eye contact, but don't stare fixedly at someone unless you are a) about to have a fight or b) in love (and in either case, make sure you do this in private).

15. Try to be a good listener rather than wittering on.

16. Double entendres aren't funny unless used ironically.

17. Don't take flirting seriously.

18. Never attempt to flirt while drunk.

19. Never flirt during board meetings or similair.

20. Be subtle – think of *Blind Date* and try to behave in manner opposite to contestants.

Having thought about flirting, conducted surveys on it, read books about it, observed it and tried it out myself – albeit disastrously – I have decided on the following three Golden Rules:

Three Golden Rules

1. Banish expectations

2. Premeditation = The Kiss of Death

3. Beware the Pungent Whiff of Desperation

It seems to me that these are the most important of all. No one can be a successful flirt unless a) they aren't expecting to get anything whatsoever out of flirting; and b) the flirtation is completely spontaneous.

Since the grim account of my dismal failure at flirting is contained earlier in this book, you might be wondering why on earth anyone should listen to me on the subject. It's a good question. But even though I have totally failed to heed my own flirting advice, perhaps other people can learn from my mistakes and be a success.

There's just time to ask...

Are You Still a Flirting Failure?

1. You are in a supermarket and spot an attractive stranger. What should you say to start off a flirtatious conversation?

a) 'These oranges are the same size as my breasts and just as firm'/'You should see my plums!'
b) 'Goodness it's busy in here today.'
c) 'What is your opinion on factory farming?'

2. Someone you've been flirting with asks for your phone number. Do you...

a) Faint.
b) Write it down in a nonchalant sort of way and hand it over.

c) Leap up and down with joy, commenting that this is the first time anyone's asked in two years.

3. Which of these is a suitable topic of conversation with someone you've just met?

a) Your minor ailments.
b) The size of your thighs.
c) Your job.

4. When you're talking to someone you don't much like, you should...

a) Remain rooted to the spot and endure it for as long as you have to.
b) Suddenly crack and start screaming uncontrollably.
c) Make a plausible excuse to end the conversation.

5. Which of the following is a flirting prerequisite?

a) Feeling happy and confident.
b) Being drunk.
c) Sexual arousal.

6. When is the best time to arrive at a party?

a) When the party's in full swing.
b) Before the booze runs out.
c) Early – you can't bear not to be punctual.

7. You notice postural echo between yourself and the person you are with. Do you...

a) Start making strange movements to see if your partner mirrors you – waving for no reason, sticking both arms out to the side, etc.
b) Feel quietly pleased with yourself.
c) Point it out to the person you're with, explaining its significance.

8. What is a good way of indicating your attraction to someone you've never met, and finding out whether they're attracted to you?

a) Glance at them for a bit longer than normal. If they return your gaze they are probably interested and if they smile they are definitely interested.

b) Tell them you fancy them and ask whether they return the compliment.

c) Wink suggestively and see whether they come running.

9. When someone you find attractive is in the vicinity, you...

a) Turn into a giggling fool.

b) Clam up completely.

c) Try not to modify your behaviour at all.

10. Which of these is the best place to flirt...

a) A party.

b) The board room.

c) In front of the telly with your invisible friend.

Answers:

1b), 2b) 3c), 4c), 5a), 6a), 7b), 8a), 9c),10a).

If you got any of the answers wrong – and perhaps even if you didn't – what can I say, you are still a Flirting Failure. Just like 98 per cent of the rest of the population and the author of this book. But don't let that stop you from trying.